Hello,
it's me

by
John Damian Di Bella

Photographs by Dave Green

Watercolor Monotype by
Phyllis Rutigliano

FORE ANGELS PRESS

ISBN 0-9658920-0-X

For Further Information Contact:
Fore Angels Press
267 Woodbury Road
Huntington, New York 11743

Manufactured in the United States of America
Peconic Companies
Mattituck, New York 11952

The just man, though he die early, shall be at rest.
For the age that is honorable comes not with the
   passing of time,
nor can it be measured in terms of years. . . .

. . .his soul was pleasing to the Lord. . . .

But the people saw and did not understand,
   nor did they take this into account.

from the Book of Wisdom
The Old Testament

Table of Contents

The work printed in this volume is printed just as John wrote it. There has been no editing. It stands on the page exactly as he placed it. There have been no changes in language, punctuation or design.

To whom it may concern

must manage words
try trying to discern
truth trapped in a verse
facts less their fiction
struggle synthetic syllables
in distressed diction

Harvest Wine

Branching tree
Creeping vine
Grapes of wrath
Harvest wine

Dead Love

Time shovels dirt
> into a grave in your garden.

Buried deep,
> the freshly dug soil

still discolored,
> makes the earth's wound more apparent.

If left untouched,
> it will fade without notice.

Dawning Day

Adagio
    in somber hues of brilliance,
    sweet musky smells of an ocean inlet,
    warm, cool, damp . . .
    feel sand between your toes,
    a light froth on the shore
    of a sandy, white beach,
    a low drone,
    the subtle resonance of a day passed,
    and the prelude to a new day.

And they will live forever

Flames of passion flicker brilliantly
in the eyes of animals.
They cry for their lover.

Wandering aimlessly through the forest,
they are not lost,
for she can always be found.

Her arms, always caressing.
Her breath, always felt.
She feeds their heated desires.

And, when weary from fatigue,
they lie to rest,
she will take them in her arms,
carrying them to her garden
where they will live forever.

Endless Night

Embrace me in your arms endless night
   My eyes close as we draw near.
You pull the blanket of darkness snugly over us.
We cling warmly until the morning light awakens . . .
   to find it was only a dream.

Tired of Weeping

I have grown tired of weeping.
My empty arms have yearned for too long.
They flail loosely by my sides.

I have grown tired of weeping.
My eyes, blurred with visions of tears,
have dried with a brightly lit day.

I have grown tired of weeping only
to look and find seeds of hope sprouting
where my scornful tears have fallen.

I have grown tired of weeping.

The Wind

The wind
collects the thoughts of the land
passes over all
like cascading water
rises and dies
like the tide
yet it can change direction
the wind

Curiosity

Curiosity
brings you near
harnessing unbridled fear
Apprehension
you hesitate
The moment passes
it cannot wait

Just a Rainy Summer Day

Rainy day . . .

    through a window

    Static in the air

    Pavement turns darker

    like spilled paint

    Umbrellas hover

    over their owners

    Rainy day halos

    teetering in the wind

    Their angels afraid to melt

    Just a rainy summer day

    through a window

Gray Day

gray day
can't play
not today

sit in bed
in my head
thoughts are wed

rain is falling
dreams are calling
weather's stalling

gray day
don't stay
you're in my way

11

Eternal Sky

Mother moon
steals away
fading light of a waning day

Father sun
wakes up bright
always redeeming morning light

Together
they live and die
in the bed of an eternal sky

Sculptures

1

Moods of the moon
   always changing
Tides of the sea
   always rearranging
the sculptures of the shore

2

The ways of life
   always cleansing
   coarse sands which
   ask for mending
Jagged stones
   polish smoother
and always beg for more

A child sees a flower . . .

A child sees a flower.
Overwhelmed by its beauty,
he is afraid to touch it.
Will it spoil in his uncontrolled grasp?
Will it wilt and die under his heavy breath?
                              He cannot touch it.

Such Fragrant Memories
To Norma Jean

Remebering visits to my grandfather's house...a rose garden in his backyard. I remember looking at the roses, budding and blooming, wilting and dying, at the many insects that the roses had fed and fostered, smiling at this silently shared relationship, sitting and wondering, wondering why anyone would cut down these roses for a dinner centerpiece or a holiday bouquet. But, what's funniest of all (at least I think so now) it was I who had severed those very roses from fibrous stems. The dirty deed done for a wine-red centerpiece or a Valentine's Day, or Mother's Day rosy bouquet. (I was fond of giving my grandmother a bouquet of roses from her own garden, I arranged them "as only a grandson knew how.")

The freshly cut roses smelled of life. They would sit in a china porcelain vase, and they would breathe their final breaths. The freshly cut roses in the china porcelain vase seemed so vibrant. They seemed to burst in deep shades of crimson red and smelled of fabled romantic love. Yet it happened too quickly that they would wilt and die, a quick faded demise. I would always keep the dried rose petals. The dried rose petals held such fragrant memories.

An Abstract Painting

An abstract painting
hanging on a wall
Lonely perception
in the minds of its audience
Constant motion
in the eyes of its painters
Universal truth
in a mirror of ourselves

Indecision

Shopping for a perspective
   aisles upon aisles
so many to choose from
different shapes and sizes
for each a different price to pay
I think I'll just browse

Passing Glances

Summer love in their eyes
Mirrored souls which never lie
Crossing paths – nothing heard
Hearts are broken without a word

Different color . . .

Different color eyes.
Different color skin.
All they have in common
     is their common sin.

New Regime

Sleepy eyes
filled with dreams
taken over by a new regime
kings and queens
fill your head
with the kingdom of your bed

Night Breed

Theirs was happiness
theirs was all the night
Breed of all the night
Their windows darkened
Yet theirs was the light
Breed of all the night
Theirs was the knowledge
Theirs was one peace
Breed of all the night

Beat

Beat the street
        with pounding feet
Play the role
        a worn out soul

Old man dies
        in a room
Mounds of money
        fill his tomb

Former lovers
        come to mourn
the lonely task
        to which he was born

Imprisoned

A boy weeps
for a love he has never had,
closes his eyes
and feels a stirring within.

Emptiness fills his chest.
A soul sighs,
heaves and then falls,
hoping to break the chains
that contain it.

A heart beats,
alone,
pounding against the prison bars,
crying to be freed
from its captor.

Attraction

A piece of iron
between two magnets–
Which does it choose?
The one that is closer.

Tug of War

Man against beast.
Conscience walks the rope,
color correlating every move.
Nobody will win
but who will lose?

Tired

Tired
Tired
Too damn tired

I need
I want
I try

      but I'm
      tired
      tired
      too damn tired

I wish
I dream
I love

      but I'm
      tired
      tired
      too damn tired

I live
I cry
I die

I was tired
      tired
      too damn tired.

Whirlpool

A swell of emotion
    fills my mind
A whirlpool of thought
    spins around in circles
    without direction
Faster and faster . . .
    consuming itself and
    subsiding in exhaustion
    without destination

Nothing

What do I leave behind?
Nothing – but words
    written on a piece of paper.
Those feelings I should have expressed.
Those things I should have said and done.
Tear stained pages in a diary
    sit on a table stand
    of an old man's death bed.

A Reminder

A boy swings from a thread
    A reminder
A baby strangled by his umbilical cord
sways like a pendulum
ticking off the agonizing seconds
    called . . . Life

A boy behind the wheel of a car
    A reminder
Engine running
a car is driven into a fog
but it does not move
The fog grows thicker
    The boy grows tired
He falls asleep behind the wheel

A note pinned to a corpse's lapel
    A reminder
A ribbon tied to a forgetful man's finger
It chimes lost memories
Yet this bell summons friends to the funeral
    of a boy

Days of Chivalry

A knight
without king or queen to serve
searches the countryside
for tales of adventure.
He seeks a maiden
born from within himself
hoping to wear her colors on his arm.
He brandishes sword and lance
galloping through meadows
on a white steed
called Dream.
He clashes with dragons
whose quests are much like his own.
They carry the same crest.
A knight lies bloodied on a battlefield
fallen prey to an enemy
called Reality.

Maybe I Will See Again

Oh God
I am blind
I cannot see
I walk cautiously
like a foolish man
trying to walk on water
I am a magician
My outstretched arms
wave in front of me
waiting for a rabbit to appear
hoping for a miracle

Sight
Oh God I beg
for sight
just for a moment
so I may plant my next step firmly
I want to see
where I have been
I must . . .
I must see
where I am going
I might fall
I am so afraid of falling

I might fall
so I will rest
I will sit down
and rest
maybe the fog will lift
A lost sailor waiting
to catch sight of a foreign land
I must sit and rest
and wait
and wait
and maybe I will see again
maybe . . .

Resurrected

Jagged lines
pen point stabbing paper
(blood pours under a scalpel's touch)
piercing words hammer their target
a reader sprawled
a book shrouds his eyes
his heart wounded
his soul bleeds
He will awaken resurrected

An Unseasoned Actor

In my mind
I write the dialogue
    for the next day.
Like an unseasoned actor
    who is too well rehearsed
    in his script,
I stumble through a lie.
    Painfully embarrassed,
I stand in front of my audience,
    stuttering and stammering.
I pray for another chance
    that may never come.

There is No Element of Surprise

My world has shrunk.
Its axis is my imagination.
Balanced on my finger
        there is no element of surprise.
The wind is my breath.
The rain – my tears.
Winter's frost – my cold touch.
Summer's heat – my nurtured passion.
A dark empty room is my space.
There is no reason to leave
        or to live.
I have chosen tomorrow's fate.

There is No Rest

Can't stand
        it
mind wanders
making a slow day
drag slower

Can't stand
        up
muscles burn
knees buckle
back aches

Can't stand
        still
I shadow box
        anxious thoughts
trying to keep on
        my toes
There is no rest

As the Years Dredge By

My love
My love
My love
      turns to dust
My love turns to dust
      as the years dredge by

My hate
My hate
My hate
      turns to wounds
My hates turns to wounds
      as the years bleed by

Crash Landing

spiraling down
miles per second
faster and faster
arms and body
plummeting lead
cannot move
cannot breathe
distorted image
warping pressure
lost consciousness
cannot wait
to kiss the ground

Noah saw a bird fly

in days gone last
as paper cut clouds billowed by
while seconds, minutes, hours passed
in the currents of an opaque sky
tumultuous waters crashed
and Noah saw a bird fly

Errata

Page 15, line 1, " Remembering..."
Page 52, line 16, "wrinkled"
Page 96, line 7, "separate"

Shell Game

Step right up.
Play a little game
of hide and seek.
Some say the hand
            is quicker
than the eye.
Well! Well!
There's only one way
to find out.
So spend a little time,
            spend a little time
(and just a little money)
and I'll give you
            a chance
to test your skill.
Who knows?
You may win.
Now look closely
            and tell me
which shell my heart lies under.

Alarm Clock

1

Lie in bed
hands behind head
elbows – angel's wings –
partners beat
a lover's treat
time's a mighty fling

2

Screaming cry
a baby dies
dreamt but never born
a foghorn clears
a rowboat steers
to the sunny shore of morn

A Boy Sat on a Wall

Behind the meadows that make the pastures
Behind the pastures that feed the farms
Behind the farms there are penned beasts
Behind the beasts there drags a plow
Behind the plow there is a newly dug furrow
Next to newly dug furrow
There are downtrodden footsteps
In front of downtrodden footsteps there is man
In front of man there is a horizon
In front of horizon there is a wall
A boy sat on the wall

A boy saw all and did not understand
The boy saw a horizon
And behind horizon he saw toiling man
With toiling man he saw scarred earth
On scarred earth grazed beast given inconsequence
Under burdened hooves fell the farms
Felled farms then to felled pastures
Felled pastures then to felled meadows
And a boy that sat on a wall looked away
To a clear bright sky

In a clear bright sky stirred a sun
The boy looked to a sun that surely faded
He looked for a moon that surely rose

He looked to a backdrop sky that shone stars
Looked to stars for taken answers
In the stars were given unanswerable questions
Yet the boy looked for more stars
The boy strained for more and wished on star
For star and more star
Bending backwards leaning to see more that hid behind
The boy fell off a wall

Scorekeeper

In the stands
he waits
for a fly ball
a souvenir
of a game
he never played
he watches
from his seat
hands hold
head's heavy thought
on his lap
a score sheet
the jotting
of a bat's diction
a score sheet
he always keeps
in a drawer
he never opens

Crows over a wheat field

Our souls
tainted black
fly above the earth
looking down
at their disfigured shadows
like crows
looking down
at a wheat field
that sways with every whisper
of the wind.
They cackle and caw
with laughter
(or is it disgust)
To the reprieve of a harvest moon

I want

To see the sun shine
and then watch it hiding
behind white, puff clouds.
Hidden till it slowly fades
behind the billowing horizon.
Doused by cleansing, rolling waters.

Orphan in Stars

A new constellation
   an orphan in stars
     parentless
       scarless
        selfless
         limitless
          endless

Tying all the Loose Ends

Life or death
heaven or hell
limbo lines of a magician's spell

day or night
light or dark
started all with a single spark

If the Scale Teeters

A scale
weighs lives
of two lovers.
They balance in harmony.
Yet if the scale teeters
either lover willingly severs
the burdens
that disturb their tranquillity.

Orchestration

Slowly the music starts to stir
All that I hear is a whir
A pitter patter to a roar
Cymbals crash like never before
The crescendo subsides as if never born
What you hear is a summer storm

Inevitable

Small pebbles
      smaller blow
dunes of sand
      taller grow
swept away into
      distant oceans
All return to the sea

Of City Streets

City streets
Sweat and fire
Pacing feet
through the mire
Summer rains wash away
the burdens of the city day

Balloons

Balloons floating together
Drift apart
Yet their strings stay entwined
Red, Green, Blue, Yellow
    They rise as one

If

if the clock runs
time skips
if there is a time
for everything
then there is time
for **nothing**

always on the run . . .

always on the run
always on the go
asking cold dark shadows
whether they be friend or foe

thus you never give

never want to take
thus you never give
empty glass of water
poured through a sieve

Two Steps

Two steps forward
One step back
Trace the trail
Resolve the track

Paradise Found
A Garden in Eden. . . through open gate

Like a youth unaging unable to remember
unaged past . . .

A garden of eden. . .

Flowers everblooming ever to grow.
Pure shades of risen rainbow never to fade.
Just blue skies never to cloud.
Summer saving sun never to cease.

Hidden and yet always seen. Lost and yet
always found. Understanding but not knowing.
Knowing and yet still not knowing. What being
real was unreal. What was and what wasn't.

There was a man. There was a woman.
When they hungered, they were silently
handfed. When they thirsted, their thirst
quenched thirst. When they tired, they had no
need for sleep.

Then and always to then: there was a man;
there was a woman . . .

and they spoke of flight.

Man: Like a bird in a cage, I am alone.
Woman: I am a feather on that bird, and I am
          alone with you.

Man:	I want more. How do I grow? How do I eat when I labor not for my own food but for the nourishing love given to an empty god.
Woman:	A selfish god who contains us in this picket fence paradise. A god who cradles us in his arms and hampers our flight for fear we may fall. A selfish suffocating god.
Man:	A god too prudent and fearful of our impending flight.
Woman:	No, No, A god too prudent and fearful of our impending fall.
Man:	Impending fall. I will fly to new heights. I will not fall. I will soar. I will soar.
Woman:	Yet wings of molded wax melt in the shadows of an exalted sun. I will not soar. Yet, I will fly. I will not soar.
Man:	You have been caged too long. You have forgotten how to soar. You. . . you cannot even fly.
Woman:	I choose not to soar, but I can fly. Like a bird in a cage, you focus your energy on unbending, oppressive bars. Yet, behind your back sways an open door. As the errant feather of a caged hawk, I will timelessly float through barred gate to the ground. Hawk in captivity, how will you soar, or even fly, without guiding tail feather?

51

Man:	Where will be my guiding tail feather?
Woman:	In my hand, on solid ground.
Man:	Will you not look to the heaven for a soaring hawk?
Woman:	I will look and pray to the heavens, not for a soaring hawk, but for you.
Man:	For me? All I have ever given you were my empty promises of far founded flight.
Woman:	No, what you have given me were your dreams, hopes and heart. What more should I ask for?
Man:	To fly. In your eyes I want to soar.
Woman:	In my eyes, I just want to find you beside me when I am tired, wrinkled and old.
Man:	In my eyes, I too want to be beside you when I too am tired, wrinked and old. I need not soar.
Woman:	You need not soar, for look; look behind you at unlocked gate.
Man:	I see but cannot believe. As a bird in a cage, I sat idly waiting to soar, * while the keys to our obstacle were ever in our hearts. Take my hand.
Woman:	I take your hand.
Man:	Walk with me through open gate.
Woman:	I walk with you through open gate.

***

*Another version reads: "As a bird in a cage, I sat idly waiting to die caged".

52

That
I Hope

That
   I hope
     my hope

      To Hope:

         to maintain found aspiration,
         when yeilding to temptation;

         to grasp that which is needed,
         and take what is conceded;

         to then carry the bent cross,
         without bending to a loss;

         to bury their blood rebel dead,
         under a battlefield of red;

         to conquer their pious crown king;

         pensive parlour talk to bring.

Hungry for a Buzz

gagging on a spoon
waiting for your man to come home
working all day
digging up a soup bone
a bone to bite
while watching digital display
with time in sight
time to play

day and night
  burning in a fire
     calling it a right
        to just get higher

not on my time
barefoot virgins bleed
tilling earth
planting seed
in the cornrows
of a hot chick
God bless you
  and me
    for being us

day and night
  burning in a fire
     calling it a right
        to just get higher

hungry for a buzz
itch scratches back
starving within
or is it without
  a forsaken man
      too stoned to shout
         shuts bloodshot eyes
           so he watches

day and night
  burning in a fire
    calling it a right
      to just get higher

hungry for a buzz
itch scratches back
starving within
or is it without
  forsaken man
      too stoned to shout
         shuts bloodshot eyes
           so he watches
day and night
      burning in a fire
        calling it a right
          to just get higher

Their Time-ing Wrong

all to do to stay awake
homeset free without a fear
requiem gibberish to break
subtle resonance in an ear

truth attain in a temple
crooked time breaks even vein
taken much aback for example
to find in all – much the same

canter to an awkward beat
music lending word to song
dancers stumble over feet
noticing their time-ing wrong

In the Name of Fun

skip rock
hit duck
living on the edge
spilled coffee cup
borrowed book
library fine
robbed bank
doin' time
making love
pair of twins
miss a baptism
original sin
imaginary lovers
wet dreams
stains on the covers
washing machines
lifting from the waist
pulled back
pack of cigarettes
smoker's hack
shortstop's error
scored run
killing innocence
in the name of fun

To Die a Viking

An ode to almighty Woden,
      as he heads a Table of Warriors
      to toast mead
      to my brother,
      as he lies bleeding
      on Battlefield of Ancients.
      Mortally wounded, he waits
      and waits for screaming Valkyries
      to carry him to Asgard,
almighty Woden's castle of the heavens.

My brother waits to die a Viking.

The Song of Almost Felled Angel

angel arrogant foresees fall
runner stumbles for his call

in the dusk of dawning night
prayers are answered out of spite

sell a soul for half the cost
pale white angel innocent lost

fails to fly, wings are clipped
grounded for the heaven trip

new on earth, a taken course
now on earth from this day forth

¹⁄₁ "Hallelujah" Phyllis Leslie Evans

Zen Riddle and I

during
 thunderclap lightning
 in an empty sky
  tightening
   on a firefly jar
and I watch

 subway hoods
 carry screwdrivers
  well shaken not stirred
   but the water is too cloudy
and I can't see the bottom

 while
 riding down a velvet highway
 meeting leather cows
  selling milk and cookies
   on satin sheets
and I hate crumbs in bed

 as
 feminine hygiene ads
 blanket the air waves and
  a soap box derby begins
   to the cheers of the crowd
and I shouldn't waste electricity

undoubtedly
    mistaken identity
    cries the Indian chief
        as last Mohicans heap praise
            and baubles and beads
and I don't watch John Wayne movies

    then
    go West
    Horace Greely son
        and where does the sun rise
            yet it has to set
and I won't eat oriental food

    betwixt
    a tear duct cathedral exit
    a church choir
        sings a requiem
            to a heavyweight of great stature
and I am not too religious

    since
    all things come to pass
    from blond to Blood
        little feet in dancing shoes
            dancing two last waltzes
and I can't dance

but there's
a lucky one in
twenty at least
if not more
naive with an open heart
and I shouldn't take his last cigarette

during
thunderclap lightning
in an empty sky
tightening
on a firefly jar
and I watch

My angel of mercy

My angel of mercy
Why do you hide from me
'fraid to show your face
or
am I too frightened to gaze
at your beauty
the incandescence of your
everyearning and insatiable soul
your distant hungry eyes
crying for a lover to accompany you
on your journey to the netherworld

Infinity Preaches
Figure Eight Sideways =s Infinity

hear me
prophets of
duration

ascribe
words in
incantation

psalm
sung song
of adulation

praise to
a Lord and
a Nation

hear me
prophets of
duration

The Nature of Being

When questioning the oracle
the stranger crosses blind eyes
quizzing lone reflectioning glass,
asking for the hidden truth,
finding hell bent broken path,
seeking, then never to fail,
portended, mended . . . ways
of praying to a golden calf.

Abide thee in shallow haze
remembering ever heard
honest words in . . . stung lies.

Now always to be now,
the stranger crosses blind eyes.

Seven Prophets of Seven Tribes Rejoiceth

Think of me during the fatal rush
passing through the forbidden land

To a plot of land
desolate plain of earth
horrid smudge of dirt
To the burial ground of my father
and the father of my father
his father and his father

To the Father of All fathers and no more
His land is sacred
His land is Holy
we are the children of the Father
we are the tenders of his holy
and sacred land of burial

He has given to us yoke and oxen
He has given to us crystal clear near stream
He has given to us O holy and sacred land
land of trusted alliance
land of a holy covenant
He has given to us All

He is the first of All Fathers
He is first and to be last
He is the Father
and we are His children
We are His children
from his loins were spawned His children
into the cradling arms
of our mother, Mother Earth

69

Everything is He, O Father guiding angel
Everything to Him from Him
Everything is He, O Father, the light of jubilant rays
Everywhere through crack and crevice to open valleys

Sing of rejoice to our heavenly Father
He is many All but One
There are none All but One
 thus sing of rejoice
 sing to the Earth
 sing to the Sky
  Sing and rejoice to your children
  to the children of your children
  the children of their children

Sing to choosing the chosen
for to them there is a holy land
for to them lies a holy and sacred land
 in the valley of honest eternity
 behind a cloud of ignorance
 a swirling dirty cloud

Unto the many the Father has given a few
seven Prophets of seven Tribes
 For to them was given a holy task
 a holy and noble deed
  to beacon the overcautious through clouded mire
  to guide the unfound through ignorant haze
  to lead the lost through blasphemous ignorant haze

Seven Prophets of seven Tribes to carry many through
eternity's threshold

To a valley
A valley that lies behind a veil of stained ignorance
To a valley of honest eternity – a valley of honest eternity
    there is truth for the sake of truth
    there is life for the sake of death
    there is death for the sake of life

In an eternal valley of truth
    All is blessed
    Blessed are the strong for they want
    Blessed are the weak for they need

For to all that is blessed is holy
For to all that is holy is blessed
All given for all – none sacrificed for none

All is One. One is All
    One is the sky
    One is the air contained within the sky

One is in taken breath
One is in given breath

Seek the One to become one
Take the One and you are One

One Father
Father is One
One Mother Earth
Mother Earth is One

One Yahweh
Yahweh is One
One Jehovah
Jehovah is One
One Allah
Allah is One
One Divine Trinity
Divine Trinity is One

One Unmentionable
Unmentionable is One

One One
One is One

The seven Prophets of the seven Tribes rejoiceth

Angel Wings

Number the wings;
darn and pair;
ready them for their
perspective owners.

If defective,
put them in
that pile
over there —
We don't want their owners
       falling
to their depths . . .

My piece of pie

Who ate my piece of pie?

   It was mine!

  Who ate it?

God damn it . . .

   That was my piece of pie!

Damn it . . .

   I'm hungry!

Where else can I get another

  piece of pie?

   It's too late now.

  I'm hungry . . .

    But where?

Scalped

Someone I know,
Maybe someone I don't know,
Asked me:
"Well, going to the show?"
     "Maybe I won't go. Got a ticket?"
"Yeah, got a no show."
     "How much?"
"How high you willing to go?"
Standing stupid,
I say I don't know.
He says:
"Want a ticket
or what?
'Cause I'll go,
you know."
Yo! Yo! After all I do want to go
see the show.

Beginning of a Dime Store Novel

She stood at the end of the dock, a Venus poised in a seductive posture, as if it had been rehearsed. As the sun ever so slowly sank into the horizon, as if apprehensive to dip into the tropical waters, all that could be seen was the silhouette of her godesslike body and her pink improvised bathing suit: probably the undergarments to a low cut black evening gown, probably by a designer with a French name. She waited patiently for a boat to shuttle her to the other side of the island where she belonged. It was late. But she waited patiently, for any improper grimace could wrinkle her face and spoil her tranquil beauty.

soapsud swimsuit

angel eyes
devil lips
sardonic grin
swaying hips
sweet breath of fire
words of sin
resurrected voice rising
above the din
fair flesh of moonlight
caressing touch of the sea
he wishes at starbright
she is his for a fee

The Storm to the Calm

tormented black Sky
still taunting pale heaven Wind
bitter tasting air

smoke gray cloud rolls cloud
blankets shining summer sun
tumbles smoking Sky

breeze blowing stronger
billowing Tree canopy
Wind wailing banshee

onto the hard Earth
water touches dusty lips
quenching dirt-dry ground

rain pelting still life
wet green leaves growing heavy
bending tree branches

spark flashes to crack
glow casting Water shadows
sharp Light fading fast

sustained noisy Light
thunderous beat on Skydrum
quickened Light dies loud

Tree leaves awakened
Water beading on greener leaves
Open to Wind and Sky

Water lapping ground
quickly swallowing cloud Water
a wet fulfilled Earth

pure sun given Light
patting Water drenched Earth dry
pure sun given Light

The Look

With a hard twist of the shoe, the cigarette was out. But wait. I stopped still in my tracks. The crumbled cigarette was narrowly smoldering in sputters of sickly smoke. I was amused so I gave it my stamp of approval. It now was out. I smiled. Smokey the Bear would be proud.

I picked my eyes up off the pavement and looked around. There was a hot, long-legged blonde at the corner waiting for Abdul and his checkered yellow camel. I thought to myself that the taxis must be real busy. I mean really busy or blind. I was thinking of asking her if she needed a lift and giving her a piggyback ride. But I didn't. She looked like the sensible type. She wouldn't have fallen for it, not twice at least.

So I gave her The Look. She reciprocated and gave me a smile. We both nodded our approval and Abdul taxied her off down Fifth Avenue. I fidgeted in my pocket for my pack and found it. I played butterfingers for a little while but caught the handle and stayed in control of my destiny. So I grabbed a cigarette, put it in my mouth, clenched it in my teeth and lit it. I took a long-faced drag and then exhaled. I released my pencil grip on the cigarette. Real casual and in one fluid motion. It dropped to the ground still lit. I felt satisfied.

Paper Shuffle

Doin the paper shuffle
    the paper shuffle
wake up early, hit the street
   crowded sidewalk
     herds in heat

Doin the paper shuffle
    the paper shuffle
uptown, downtown
    go to work
on time to office, earn a perk

Doin the paper shuffle
    the paper shuffle
proofread, xerox, even fax
  pens and pencil
    pads to stack

Doin the paper shuffle
    the paper shuffle
till next morning, yer comin' back
Help keep The Company in the black

Where Were You
When the Bombs Were Falling . . .

Where were you when the sky was crying,
Where were you when your friends were dying?
Living your life fantasy free –
No one to tell you that your dreams can't be.
Where were you when the bombs were falling,
Where were you when I was calling?
Where was I when your tears first bled?
Where was I when the water was red?
Drowning in a sea of fate –
Only clinging to your hate.

Playing with a Handicap

I

To see the devil and see the sun
One looks at the ground and the sky
And acknowledges that they are one.

To see the self and see the other
One looks in the mirror
And calls Me brother.

II

To be concerned with the truth
and what it opposes is one and the same.
To flip a coin and pray that it lands on edge
is all but a handicap of the game.

You never call

I've been up and down
        that mountain
Waited for the Lord to
        toss me a bone
I've waited for the Lord
        to call on me
But I haven't got a phone

Now I've waited
        waited for your love to fall
Now I've waited for
        you darling
Wait for love that
        never called

See you get your loving
        from the drug store down
                the block
Getting your loving
        from every dog with a bark

Now I've waited
        waited for your love to fall
Now I've waited
        for you darling
                but you never call

It's Been So Long

It's been so long
    since I've been down to you

It's been so long
    since I've gotten to touch you

But the days go on
    and I am still a-counting

Mustang in my head
    is being mounted

It's been so long
    since I've gotten to kiss you

The darkened night
    framing a neon sign

A greyveined highway
    lined with spruce and pine

It's been so long
    since I've gotten to taste you

Wet coffee grounds
    and a smoking ashtray

Lone wolf on the prowl
    with duck feet of red clay

Strength

You're so strong
> You can kick up my spit

I'm so strong
> I can walk away

You're so strong
> I can hesitate

You're so strong
> You can hold back your tears

I'm so strong
> I can cry

Cage Yet

tried to tire
yet too tired to try
too little yet too much
too early
yet too late
hunger to eat
yet food fails to fill hunger
success story
yet a failure
to love
yet to hate
seek an answer
yet what is the question

In Alphabet City

street hoods in war paint pass out
    leather bundles of calling cards;
electric garage bands play
    funeral dirges;
to the service of zombies;
    itchy music
chases a derelict
    to find pocket lint,
swatches of litter-trace;
    a whirlwind . . .
a rolling sidewalk shadows
    workboots and sneakers worn thin;
a story book supermercado,
    leans at every corner;
and a sandblasted brick tenement
    frames
    a brisk fall scene.

I Want a Tattoo

I want a tattoo . . . something not too pretentious. Cause when I'm taking my new black Harley (of course with a teardrop gas tank with a sweet red rose painted on it) across country, I don't want to fall into disfavor with my new biker friends.

Something simple, but that makes a clear and concise statement. An ex. Definitely the letter X. On my arms. Not on the left or the right arm, but on both. Yeh, definitely both. I would then live in harmonious balance.

Shopping for a Tattoo

Wow! You sure gotta neat tattoo on your arm.
Boy! Looks kinda like a demon hound from Hell.
That's amazing! I've been looking all over for a
tattoo like that; something that personifies the
angst and ennui one experiences when one comes
of age. And if I might ask, out of the sincerest
curiosity,why **did** you get that particular tattoo?
Sure, sure. Fair enough.
You're right, by golly!
It does look mean and nasty.
Well then, I guess I'll mosey along and go off on
my merry way.
But before I do, I'd like to mention that
that is just such a neat tattoo on your arm,
such a neat tattoo.

Hip and Hop Rap

jungle rhythm to the beat
shake your booty in your seat
side to side, swing your hips
this record here never skips

on and on till the dawn
shake your booty, you can't go wrong
bustin loose, bring down the house
do it like you talk about

Hip and Hop, till you drop
bouncing hard, won't ever stop
bring it forth, bring it back
my time, night time, always black

can front me, front another
know it now, never front a brother
strangle hold, then here you fall
take a quarter, make momma call

back boy now, learn the dance
friction heat, burn your pants
needs and wants, posse takes
trouble you want, posse makes

The Philosopher King

The philosopher king
>   doesn't know how to sing.
He knows all these truths,
>   but he can't sing the blues.
He guides all men's way.
>   But guitar he can't play.

The philosopher king
>   doesn't know how to sing.
When the noblemen came,
>   they found out much the same:
>   that the knowing old goat
>   can't hold a note,
>   that the knowing old goat
>   can't hold a note.

Cordial Sherry

have a sip
of cordial sherry
sweet drunkeness
heated in front of hearth

       flickering silhouettes
       shadow wrestling
       in the heat
       of winter's rage

have a sip
of cordial sherry
sweet drunkeness
heated in front of hearth

       jumping flames
       pulsate on command
       to the meter
       of heart rhythm

have a sip
of cordial sherry
sweet drunkeness
heated in front of hearth

       Bearskin lovers
       embrace jaded
       cliches of
       unforseen love

Last Night

Last night a banshee whispered in my ear. She told me; What to do and what not to do. Where to go and when to walk. When to crawl and when to run. She told me she cared, last night. And if she didn't tell me with her words then she did so with her phantom eyes. We did not want to seperate from one another last night. Alone, when we stand alone-without one another, our lives are cold and clammy. Yet when we're together, our hearts are kindling in the hearth of our soul. I could have told her I loved her last night. I should have told her I loved her and that we would never part. What's funniest of all, last night a banshee whispered in my ear....

a dog leashed to a tree . . .

a dog leashed to a tree
a fish in a bowl
a mouse in a maze
a bird in a cage
a pig penned
horses in a corral
a prisoner shackled to a wall
a cripple in a wheelchair
lions in a zoo
car in a garage
a tool unbought
whale beached on a shore
sailboat without a mast
a man alone

I was told to be like a leaf in the wind . . .

I was told to be like a leaf in the wind
a leaf in the wind
    not held to a branch
    not alienated by fateful circumstance

a leaf in the wind
    hovers over all the branches
    at times gets snagged on an inconsequential twig

but the wind returns to its untendered child
    holds the leaf in His arms
    and carries it away
    so he may fly again

the wind does not navigate the leaf on its course
    He just fills the leaf's sail
    and the leaf just floats onto his destiny

Hello it's me

Hello it's me
who else
Don't hang up
not yet
I have something to say
or have I said too much already

click

I guess I have –